As the Lies Turn

By: TiAnna Coleman

As the Lies Turn

Dedication

I give honor to God who is the head of my life. I give special thanks to Him because this book would not have come to fruition without Him. I want to thank my husband, Anthony Coleman, who gave me the privilege to write this book and let the world in on our marriage. Without the struggles, trials and tribulations we wouldn't be standing here today with a voice reaching out to your hearts. I would like to thank my friend Jessica who has inspired me to help others with this piece and BooksfortheSoul

As the Lies Turn

LLC for inspiring others to write their own story. I personally would like to thank my favorite cousin Sonia for staying up all night and encouraging me to finish this great piece. My cousin Shakeita for helping me at the last minute without asking any questions. I would like to thank myself for being obedient and for not stopping even when I didn't understand how God was going to release As the Lies Turn. I would like to thank everyone who were there to witness our ups and downs and never taking sides. I know it may seem as though some may judge and take sides but there are 3 sides to the story. Every Marriage is

3

As the Lies Turn

different and will not go through what we

have endure in the first couple of years

being married but don't be discouraged

about marriage or getting married. If God

allowed us to get through it, He will

certainly do the same for you.

As the Lies Turn

Foreword

TiAnna Coleman is an Extraordinary and courageous young woman. I have witnessed TiAnna encourage others in an effective way. I asked her, how do you know how to love the unlovable and to go the extra mile even when you are running out of gas? She stated that she has been unlovable and messed up, but God. God has loved me in my broken state, so I love others back in return. TiAnna loves to celebrate others. She is a friend, mother, sister and wife. Her love flows freely to all that encompasses her

As the Lies Turn

path. She gives from the heart. She is

thoughtful and kind. Her personality is a

balance of sweet and tangy. She speaks her

mind. She apologizes quickly and she thinks

things through. As the Lies turn will give

other marriages hope to survive and to

continue the journey towards a committed

and faithful union.

Jessica LaToya Johnson
BooksfortheSoul LLC

As the Lies Turn

Copyright @ 2019
TiAnna Coleman
ALL RIGHTS RESERVED

As the Lies Turn

Table of Contents

(7 years of completion)

As the Lies Turn

Love at First Sight

A late tiresome night as I vacuumed the hotel suite, one of my employee's phones rang, I said to her, "Now, Shantay you know the policy here, no phones allowed while on the clock." She asked if I could answer her phone while she continued to dust the suite, I obliged to her request and, I answered the call. It was a male at the other end, so I gave the phone to my employee/ friend, "chuckling" about the comment of the phone policy. As she got the phone her brother

9

As the Lies Turn

Anthony asked, "Who is that?" she replied, "My supervisor, TiAnna with her big-headed self." Anthony asked, "How does she look? Does she have a big booty?" I laughed as I heard the comment. Shantay said, "My brother said you should "call him." I got the number and haphazardly I called what seemed to be the perfect stranger. We talked for nights and nights finding ourselves falling asleep to be awaken to the voices of each spirits as we entwined with a deep connection of conversations reaching beyond the surface of the soul. I couldn't wait to meet this love of mine as our telephone conversations grew

As the Lies Turn

to the core of my heart and up to the point it was time to meet face to face. As Anthony seemed to be hesitant to see me, the phone calls began to be short and quick, and I had no clue for his distance. The next morning, I got a call from Shantay, my cell phone rang from my bedroom as I was brushing my teeth in the shower trying to rush to work because one of my employees called off and I had to cover the shift. Looking in the mirror staring at myself, saying, "What is wrong with Anthony and his communication we haven't stayed on the phone like we use to? Just then, my phone rang. "Hello"

As the Lies Turn

Shantay said "TiAnna you know Anthony

been locked up?"

COMMUNICATION

James 1:9

"It is better to listen than to speak"

As the Lies Turn

I exhaled, feeling relieved from all the confusion that had begun to captivate my mind, and wondering if he was still interested in me. After I worked the exhausted day shift, I was released from my menial day of burdensome chores. Shantay sent me a text saying, "TiAnna come to my sister house, I replied "Girl I'm tired. My feet hurt, and people kept calling off the day, thereby leaving me to pick up the slack." Shantay said "Please big head." I responded, "Okay, text me the address." As Shantay texted me my phone rang and it was my boo, Anthony. As I picked up, with my heart smiling physically and emotionally, he

As the Lies Turn

asked me to come see him at his sister Michelle's house. He said "Shantay sent you the address already so come on." As I began to drive closer to the destination I was filled with butterflies and deep throbbing burst of nervousness that had me shaking and biting my nails. I pulled up to the destination and walked into a house full of company where I only recognized two people and everybody else just strangers. As Shantay meets me in the kitchen, she said loudly, "YOU KNOW YOU SEE HER IN HERE!" As Anthony came to meet me for the first time, his smile was the first thing that greeted me, and he had a mouth full of golds. I was blown away

As the Lies Turn

by his swag and long dreads that had me mesmerized as our eyes locked and I could off have sworn our energy merged into two. This was love at first sight, I was blown away by his charisma and humor, Anthony was sweeter in person than he was on the phone. He embraced me with affection that I never had in a long time, and I felt whole and complete. I was truly in love, and I was appreciated.

As the Lies Turn

COMMUNICATION

Proverbs 18:21

"Life and Death are in the power of the tongue"

As the Lies Turn

As the night began to travel into seconds,

minutes and hours, Anthony began to caress

my shoulders. I began to be fearful of the

time, my curfew was at midnight. I told him

I will see him tomorrow. He said, "Okay

you haven't even let me finish the massage."

I ran out giggling to make it home to

shower, and I found myself overtaken by

this handsome man. He was more than

enough for me, and everything my heart

longed for. I and the perfect man spent

countless of time together. It was not long

after the shower he had called and we talked

for hours and sometimes, we had nothing to

say but just that thought on being on the

As the Lies Turn

phone made us happy. You know that high school phone conversations were two love birds fall asleep while the other one snores. Yes, that was us, but it didn't matter to me because I finally found someone with the same interests as myself. I lucked up on that man and I was glad to have been the one that answer that phone call. Who would have known that we would have been together till this day?

COMMUNICATION

"Do not talk to kill, talk to heal, words hurt more than any physical weapon."

Secrets

Who would have thought when getting

married it would be chaotic? I didn't believe

it would but getting married after 7 months

of dating, it all began. While dating there

were no signs of desertion. We were so in

love that we yearn for each other 24/7.

When you see him, you will see me and vice

versa? We were two Aries that wanted to be

together. On February 14, 2012, my love

decided to propose to me after 7 months of

being together. We were talking about

As the Lies Turn

marriage just 5 months into our relationship. His proposal was not an ordinary proposal that you see today. It was an intimate him and I in our bedroom and he asked me to be his wife. Of course, my answer was "Yes" since I was so deeply in love with him. How could I say no when I didn't have any reason too? After being engaged a couple days Anthony stated he wanted to get married right away. I looked at him stunned and was like "Are you serious"? His reply was yes, and I replied I was thinking like a year or so down the line, but that was not what he had in mind. His right of way was months and his wish came true.

As the Lies Turn

He told me he was leaving everything in my hands and whatever I came up with was just okay with him. He should have never told me that I had everything picked out that night from the place, color, dresses, songs, menu, bridesmaids and groomsmen. I didn't waste any time since he said he was ready. On April 14, 2012 was the day we decided to become ONE just after two months of being engaged. Planning a wedding on my own was a big headache, but I enjoyed it because it was my vision and if anything went wrong, I was the one to blame. Our wedding was inexpensive and beautiful just two months of planning. Our wedding was

As the Lies Turn

one the happiest days of my life because I

became a wife, which is something every

girl dream to become.

As the Lies Turn

HONESTY AND TRUST

Ephesians 5:25

" For husbands this means love your wives, just as Christ loved the church. He gave up his life for her"

As the Lies Turn

It rained all day until the time the ceremony started. I was happy it rained because I remember reading that if it rains on your wedding day, it signifies good luck. I guess it was good luck because we made it official. I prayed to God right before walking down that aisle that if it was meant to be, let it be a successful marriage. The ceremony started late because I was crying, and I couldn't believe I was getting married at the age 25. I got the butterflies out right before that door opened for me to walk down to Jennifer Hudson "Giving Myself". Our Ceremony had such a great turn out from both sides of our family and friends.

As the Lies Turn

We enjoyed that day like it was our last. In God's house we made a vow to God and Mrs. Fields (Officiant) to have and to hold, for better or worse, for richer, for poorer, in sickness and in health, to love and cherish, till death do us part. I had meant every word with all my heart and I sure thought he did too. I believe that my husband did as well at that moment, but that's where the lies began. After being married a couple months there came dishonesty, lies, lack of communication, disloyal and overall pure weakness. I thought getting married supposed to be a beautiful feeling. I dreamed of a perfect marriage, family and husband

As the Lies Turn

and got the opposite when it came to marriage and husband. My husband will play it cool and I will go with the flow. I didn't want to believe that the things I saw on television would happen to me. Maybe because I was in denial because I just got married. Therefore, any and everything he was doing was justified, well I thought it was. My husband would lie to me and I will believe every word that came out his mouth. When I met him, he was in church playing for the Lord, so I thought I had a good Christian man that knows and love the lord. In the beginning was love at first sight and we fell deeply in love with each other. I thought that love will transfer over in our marriage, but it expired for some time. I thought I was a perfect woman who had everything together,

As the Lies Turn

and so how can someone mistreat a woman like
myself. I cook, cleaned, worked, satisfied his
sexual needs, loved him, supported him, gave him
attention and always communicated. Well, I was
wrong because I was picturing how my life will go,
but instead I got the opposite what I dreamed. I
started questioning myself if I was truly doing
everything that I needed to do to satisfy his needs.

As the Lies Turn

I knew I didn't do anything wrong but love him for him. I asked myself and prayed to God asking, did my husband get cold feet after we got married? Did Anthony make a mistake when we got married? Did Anthony feel like I was like one of his ex's? All these questions would keep playing in my head. After so long of not trusting him I would question his every move but wouldn't get an honest answer to save my life. If he answers I knew it was probably a lie, but I would still believe it because I was deeply in love with that man. Why I believed it, I couldn't just answer that aloud just in my head. I would cry all day and night because I would get emotional just thinking the "what if." What if he is cheating? What if he is loving another woman? What if I was never the woman he wanted to marry? What if he is giving another woman what he

As the Lies Turn

supposed to be giving to me? These

questions will have my mind racing every

day. I started to question myself again, but

why when I was the one who took the "I

Do" serious. I would get advice and listen to

my aunts on my dad side who have been

married for 10 years plus. They never

judged and never brought up what we talked

about to other people. I confided in them

because they always gave me good advice

whether I would accept it or not. I also heard

other couples who have been married a long

time once told me the first 7 years are the

hardest years if you let it be. I didn't want to

believe it. I was like, marriage is a piece of

As the Lies Turn

cake, but nope I was all the way wrong. All marriages and persons are not the same. Being married after 7 months, we never got to know each other physically, emotionally, mentally and spiritually. The conversation never was brought up about our goals, and the typical questions couples ask before pursuing a relationship. Our relationship was straight forwarded. We were so caught up and in love with the fact we had so much common. We both love God, church, sports, hot wings, cheese fries, homebodies, sex, and jokes and were family oriented. Who wouldn't want to be with someone with the same similarities? That should be a reason to

As the Lies Turn

love a person, but boy I was caught up.

Caught up in the fact this man would wrong

me, and I accepted every flaw and make

excuses for him to justify everything he was

doing ok. I thought I could call some of my

married friends to vent to but that backfired.

Some will listen and wish the best for me,

then you had that one that was always

negative no matter what it was. The one that

was negative would just say you need to

leave him because you deserve better. Yes! I

deserved better, but what kind of so-called

friend will advise you leave him. She

couldn't wait for him to do something so she

could call me to tell me. The friend who

As the Lies Turn

always wanted everyone to believe her

marriage was great to throw it in your face,

but it wasn't as she seems it to be. A friend

that's says a person can't change. I would

believe everything this so-called friend

would say and I would be thinking like her

and not for myself. I would approach him

and question him about what others will tell

me even if I didn't feel it in my guts. I

would say I heard but wouldn't tell him who

said it and we'll begin to argue because I

wouldn't be open to how he would feel. At that

moment, I would cry because

HONESTY AND TRUST

As the Lies Turn

Colossians 3:9

"Do not lie to each other, since you have taken off your old self with its practices."

As the Lies Turn

I let someone else dictate my marriage before, I had proof. My husband was always at church, so I wouldn't think of anything because when we met that was where he was always at. I didn't think I needed to go to church with him every Sunday to see if he was doing anything. After a year being married, I would get signs and my female intuition kicked in. He would come home late than usual, and his ring wouldn't be on his finger because he stated he was playing basketball and he didn't want to lose it. He would turn his phone off or ringer on silent, but I didn't think anything of it because when we first met, he was always at church.

As the Lies Turn

So, I thought that was the reason. He had a
Face book account but wouldn't
acknowledge he was married on his profile.
He wouldn't compliment me anymore, we
didn't go out as much and he became quiet
and secretive. I asked myself what happen to
the man I fell in love with? The one that
made me smile every day, the man that
loved on me no matter where we were at?
Where did that person go? People knew he
was doing wrong all along except the person
he was married too. I get it! Their loyalty
lies with him and not me because I didn't
know or try to get know his friends. It seems
like they will praise him for what he was

As the Lies Turn

doing instead of letting him know the truth.
He's married and has a wife and kids at
home. The wife that stood at the altar to say,
"I do". His friends knew what type of person
and wife I was, but that didn't matter to
them. He could do anything under the sun,
and they wouldn't say a word. One thing
was certain; I did my part as a wife and a
mother. I was honest and faithful the entire
time he was acting up. The thought about
cheating crossed my mind, but two wrongs
don't make it right, so I never did. The
thought about it would be roaming in my
head and I would talk myself out of it. I felt
like getting back at him wouldn't prove

anything, but more hurt. Hurt because the man I married had decided to take my love for granted. I would try and converse with other men, but my heart and soul wouldn't allow me too. I was a great woman who respected myself and marriage and knew everything will be okay. I just prayed to my God until I couldn't anymore.

HONESTY AND TRUST

As the Lies Turn

"Without honesty there is no trust, make it your effort to be honest so trust can be granted"

As the Lies Turn

I asked God Why me? God answered and said," You prayed for that man." I had to think of what I prayed for. God answered me and said, "You prayed for a husband, but not what you wanted in a husband." Then, I knew I had made a mistake. I should have prayed for a Godly man, provider, protector, faithful and respected husband. I prayed again and I prayed to God to heal him and delivered him from anything that's hindering him to love me like I should be loved. During those rough patches, I continue to stay prayed up no matter what I was going through. I ask God to remove him if he's not meant for me. I didn't want to be

As the Lies Turn

in this marriage if I had to question him
every day. I didn't get married to get a
divorce and I didn't get married just to say I
was married. I got married to my husband
because I thought I found my heart and soul
mate. After, being disappointed I tried to
just focus on myself and my children.
Although, the children didn't see anything
we were going through because I chose not
to have any type of disagreements around
them. I knew at some point that my marriage
was over. I would put him out and he will
leave without putting up a fight and I would
just cry until I feel asleep. At that waken
moment, I knew he didn't love or care for

As the Lies Turn

this marriage anymore. When he would leave, I didn't think he wouldn't not answer his phone because we had kids together. He didn't care what I was calling for and he didn't care to answer. I would blow his phone up until I was tired of calling. I have never been this way about a man or relationship before. Was that love the reason I took so much from him or was I just being stupid? People probably would call me stupid, but I didn't care what others thought about me or my marriage. I did listen to other opinions whether it was good or bad, but now I knew that whatever decision I made, it would be what my heart will allow.

As the Lies Turn

At that moment, I knew I had some issues
that I never talked about because I thought I
would be over it by now. I knew I needed to
let a lot go from my past to move on and
save my marriage. I decided to go to
counseling for myself. I knew I needed to
talk to someone who doesn't know anything
about me, and what I needed to try to get
past this hurt. I went in with the intentions to
let my hurt and pain out without being
judged. I release it and I cried like I never
cried before because I knew I had so much
in my heart but didn't know it was that deep.
Before counseling, my husband and I will
fight like cats and dogs. Arguments after

As the Lies Turn

arguments, and it didn't matter what it was
we were arguing about. It was about me and
what I wanted and not how he felt. I didn't
express how I felt to my husband because I
would assume, he knew how I felt. I didn't
open up to him about my past, so he didn't
know what I encountered as a child. I didn't
want to bury him with all my worries, but I
didn't ask if he cared either. Being fatherless
from my younger years took a toll on my
life. I would disrespect my husband because
I felt like he was just like my daddy. My dad
who is no longer with us (RIP) raised me to
the age 10. I was a daddy's girl at some point and
was be the happiest girl in the world until he left me

As the Lies Turn

for a woman and our relationship never remained
the same again. I would cry to my dad, for another
moment to build our relationship. I wanted that love
back, but he seemed like he didn't care anymore. If
I was ever question whether he loved me I would
have said NO. A father would never leave his child
to be with someone. A father would never let
someone come between him and his child. A father
wouldn't allow himself to go days without talking
to his child. Being the only child, I yearned for that
love from my father. It hit me hard that my father
just didn't care and for that moment I stopped
caring. I would think my husband was like my
father in many ways. I would say to myself that my
husband can't love me because my father didn't. He
probably did, but he just didn't show it to me. After
counseling I felt relieved that a burden was lifted

As the Lies Turn

off my shoulders. I realized I couldn't let my father dictate how my marriage will be. I had to realize that my husband is not my father and does not have anything in common with him except being a man. When my husband and I got married, I couldn't have that moment of having my dad walked me down the aisle. I was hurt due to disappointments, selfishness and lack of love. So why should I feel to need to ask him to be a part of my special day? I always wanted that moment to come and all I ever wanted was to have that father and daughter dance, but my dreams died a long time ago with our relationship. Our special day, I had someone very special to me walk me down the aisle. My uncle, Orlando a man who's been there through it all and never left my side. He was still there since birth even when my dad left. When I asked my uncle, I

As the Lies Turn

knew it was the right thing to do, I was happy he said yes. I looked at my uncle like a father figure, although I knew I had a father. I didn't take that away from my father but giving respect to the man that held me down. I love the relationship my uncle and I have. A relationship I dreamed to have with my father as an adult.

As the Lies Turn

Nightmare from Hell

Sleeping alone some nights and having some of the craziest dreams had me scared. I was scared to the point that I did not think our marriage was going to ever work and down the road to a divorced. I knew what I wanted for our marriage but was it the same for him? Divorce was not an option because I always believe that two people can make it work if they work on it. I would remember being brought up by older couples and how they would work through their differences to make their family work. I had that in my mind that although we been through some ups and downs that we were so in love to make our marriage last. One night I was playing around on an old phone of his that didn't

49

As the Lies Turn

have any services or internet; I came across some
horrific message on his Face book messenger. He
was about to get out the shower when I discovered
that a married woman would send her private parts
to a married man like him. I believed they were
involved with each other, but I didn't know for sure
at that moment. What kind of woman would be so
open to send a stranger her private area? It rang a
bell that they must have messed around in the past
to be so comfortable to share nude pictures. I was
one of those women who did not go through phones
or anything if I did not have any reasons too. I was
so mad that I bust open the bathroom door where he
was drying off from his shower and had the phone
in my hand. The look on his face was so priceless
because he had known I knew something. I said,
"Oh that's what you're doing we letting a woman

As the Lies Turn

send their private area and you couldn't even say anything to me about it. He knew at that very moment I was about to kill him, but he couldn't say anything at that time because I was furious. I was wondering what he was thinking, but I bet he thought his life was over. Therefore, I didn't want to be in the same house as him that night, and so I told him I will leave to clear my mind. He decided to leave, and I stayed with my children. Being up all night and thinking why? Why would a married woman who have a husband and kids send a married man her private parts? Why does he think it was okay to accept it and not tell his wife? Why both are married if they decide to act single? So many questions I pondered on that made me not sleep at all that night.

As the Lies Turn

PATIENCE

1 Corinthians 13:4

"Love is patient, love is kind. It does not envy, it does not boast, it is not proud"

As the Lies Turn

I was so sick to my stomach that I couldn't get myself together because I thought after the secrets at first, we were over the lying, cheating and the disrespect. After talking to him I decided to contact her and ask her what was going on. You would think that church people would have it together, but nope you are singing for the Lord and sinning at the same time. I contacted her and of course I knew I wouldn't get any truths at that moment from her until I threated to tell her husband. I asked her how she would feel if I send to her husband pictures of my private area. She had started pleading her case and I couldn't understand why she would let a married man to manipulate her, but then again, I told her "You are grown so he couldn't have manipulated you?" How can you hurt another woman knowing he was married? Why wait to get

As the Lies Turn

married and cheat? She was crying and saying sorry
and asked me to forgive her. I replied "You are
only sorry that you got caught. "I said I'll forgive
you after I whooped your ass." I knew at that
moment it wasn't worth it, and so I prayed, prayed,
and prayed. I knew I had to let it go, but as bad as I
wanted to kill both, I had my children to take care
of. Emotions were all over the place and when I
thought my trust was building up, it died again. I
forgave him so many times and couldn't understand
why. He would come back saying he want his
family to work and that he's sorry and he will never
do it again. I will believe his lies and take him back.
So much hurt and you wouldn't understand until I
get back at you, but I was not that woman. I love
my husband and marriage so much that I just let go
at that moment. Every Sunday I would be so mad

As the Lies Turn

that he was going to church knowing he would see that woman again. I didn't attend church often and I didn't believe I had to so people could know that he was married. The church people knew he was married but him" Chuckling". Walking around like he was a single man. The women in church would love that attention knowing he was married. Yea I didn't fault them but at the same time don't speak to me when you see me and you doing foul things with my husband. I will have several dreams about the whole situation and I often took it to work me with. I let my household take over how my work day would be. I will catch an attitude with everyone knowing they didn't have anything to do with what I was dealing with. I let it get the best of me every day. I took some time and I had to prepare myself everyday when I step a foot out my house. I had to

As the Lies Turn

call my Best Friend, Shay, to calm me down at that moment. She would know exactly what words to say to me.

PATIENCE

As the Lies Turn

Ephesians 4:2

"Be Completely humble and gentle; be patient, bearing with one another in love"

As the Lies Turn

She was always encouraging and letting me know I am here for whatever decision I make. She never said I should leave my husband or anything negative. She will ask me if I had talked to him about the situation and would reply no and that I rather cool down before I approach him avoid being mad with him. She said give it a couple days and have your thoughts together then approach him. I listened to her advice, but deep down I wanted to destroy him in every way. I let my anger and immaturity get the best of me because I started blasting our relationship on Face book for the world to know. I was hurt and disappointed, and so I didn't care what others would think. Most of my friends and family on Facebook would tell me to take the post down. I kept it up because I knew someone would have showed him what I said. I was

As the Lies Turn

ready for whatever came my way including outsiders, family friends, and his family. I bashed him over and over because at that time it made me feel better because I got to release some emotions I had been feeling for some time. Was it right? At that moment yes it was, but when I look back, I can see how I embarrassed myself because we were married and had children together. I then deleted every post I ever made and just prayed about the situation. I knew at that time I was not over him. I loved him so much that at the thought that he wronged me, I would ignore it just to be back with him. Yea most people look at me crazy and talked bad about me but understand you all didn't get married to him, I did, and whatever I chose to do I do without any permission from anyone.

PATIENCE

"Patience is the key to acceptance"

As the Lies Turn

I found myself talking to God and laying all

my problems down to him because that was

only person that would not judge me. I

prayed to God to strengthen my heart and

mind that I will walk by faith no matter what

the decision we decide at this point. I was

distraught at the fact that after a year or, so

we would be divorced. I came to realization

that sometimes some people must separate

to get back to themselves. In my head I was

ok, but deep down I was so sick that I would

call off work because I felt like I was no

good to work. At that moment I knew I had

to get myself together. During that night I

would toss and turn and think about the

As the Lies Turn

things I been through and wondering if he

was still entertaining those women. I would

have dreams after dreams and questions

after questions. I decided to not let someone

have so much power over me to be losing my

mind and missing work. So, I began to pray for a

change behavior what I was praying for and he

change tremendously. No questions had to be asked,

no worries, no arguments, and no more sleepiness

nights

As the Lies Turn

Well some people may have guess that after all I've been through, I would have decided to divorce my husband and move on with my life. That was not in God's plan for me. My husband made his mind up that his wife and family was all he needed. God placed me in his life for a reason and that was to help him so he could help himself. I never gave up on him because I would feel as everyone else if I did give up on him. That's when the lies turn. You all may have

As the Lies Turn

thought as the lies turned it would consist of all negativity, but the lies turned to truth. He had change for himself to become a better husband, provider and father. I didn't force him because I came to realization that no matter what I say or do, if a man doesn't want to change, he certainly won't. I prayed to God for a changed man and ask to heal him in every way and remove any demons that is hindering him to grow. I stepped back and allowed God to work it out for us. When he was finally done being immature, he realized what he was doing was hurting the person that loved him dearly. I didn't give in as fast as he thought I would even though I forgave him. I voiced my opinion that we have to talk and figure what will work best for our marriage. We laid everything out on the table, and I proceeded to let him know what I

will allow and will not. That was the first mistake

because we never talked about what we both wanted

in a marriage. I explained to him how I felt and how

everything he had done hurt me.

TIME

Psalm 90:12

"Teach us to number our days, that we may gain a heart of wisdom"

As the Lies Turn

He agreed that he was wrong and apologized
never does it again. I stated to him that he
probably didn't know he was doing it
because he was used to treating women
wrongly and so he thought it was right to
mistreat his wife. I told him if he should try,
I will give my best as well and that he had to
help me to help us. I couldn't be the only
person in the marriage that's always trying,
rather it takes two. I gradually asked him
over and over some questions to reassure if
this marriage was what he really wants. He
replied, "I wouldn't be here and fighting if I
did not want this marriage to work." I just
didn't want to make the same mistake again

As the Lies Turn

believing and listening to his lies. Therefore, at that moment, I knew he wanted the marriage to be saved because his behavior became different; he changed his number, created a new Facebook account, and would put me first. He brought back hope that I was long was dreaming for. When his actions showed more, that was how I knew I had fallen back in love with my husband. Anyone can say anything about change, but actions speak louder than words. No doubt in my mind, and I thank God for letting me stay to help him. I helped him because I prayed for him not to change for me but to become a better person. I knew he had the

As the Lies Turn

potential to, but he just didn't believe in

himself. He didn't believe that someone like

me can actually love and be in love with him.

He didn't think he can make someone happy, being

an awesome father and husband. He doubted

himself so much throughout his life, and all he

knew was failure until he met me. I gave him hope

that I was there to help him and not judge him for

his past.

TIME

"Time is more precious than money, be careful how you spend it"

As the Lies Turn

Anthony knew that he couldn't keep hurting the people that stood by his side after all his wrong doings. When you're constantly in hurt you push people away that care for you. I was his motivator, supporter, and listener even though I was hurting. We can't never force anything that's not meant to be. That moment, I love me again because I made time to love myself which was deeper than wanting a man to love me. I constantly told myself that I am beautiful, brave, smile, don't give up and know your worth. I will conquer no matter the circumstances and I reminded myself that no man deserves all of me if he can't give me all of him. I would

As the Lies Turn

look in the mirror and ask myself the type of

woman I would want my girls to become. I

had my mind set in place to stopped

nagging, cursing at him, being mean and

being disrespectful toward him. We learned

to talk about our problems out before it will

occur. I learn to communicate, listen and

learn to let a man be a man. I didn't

understand that at first because I was always

independent and did everything on my own.

Reality sunk in why be in a marriage if you

can't compromise what your significant

other may want and need? Reminding

myself that he is there to help, but it was

hard for me to adjust for a long time.

As the Lies Turn

Adjusting to the fact to let him take lead and
be the head of the household. I had to adapt
to change and accept the outcome to become
a better wife. I had flaws that I always
thought was good intentions, but they were
not good in the eye of my husband.

As the Lies Turn

TIME

As the Lies Turn

2 Corinthians 6:2

*"In the time of my favor
I heard you, and in the
day of salvation I helped
you, I tell you now is the
time of Gods favor"*

As the Lies Turn

Surrender

My marriage turned for the better, and that's why we owe everything to God.

We surrendered our faults and prayed to God to keep us as one, and that no one or anything should hinder us to love on each other. I had to become submissive to my husband and allowed him to be the head of the household. I let my pride to the side and let him be the man to lead our house as he should have from the beginning. We both gave up selfishness, complaining and putting one another last.

As the Lies Turn

FORGIVENESS

As the Lies Turn

1 John 1:9

"But if we confess our sins, he is faithful and just to forgive us our sins and cleanse us from everything we've done wrong"

As the Lies Turn

Believing in God and allowing him to work us out was the best thing that happens to us. Sometimes I will lose faith because I wanted everything to move when I did. God has a timing and his timing was perfect. We both had to grow apart to come back together to be one. During trials and tribulations God dealt with us together and apart. He had to separate us to lead us back to a happy place. God allowed our hearts to heal before letting us make a mistake again. During those difficult times, I prayed and cried because I was in a dark place.

FORGIVENESS

Matthew 6:14-15

For if you forgive men their trespasses, your heavenly father will also forgive you.

As the Lies Turn

Coming out that dark place and coming back into sunlight made me realized it was time for us to become best friends again. Despite the wrong doings God made a way to let my husband and I forgive what we've been through. God had a purpose for us, and I knew at that moment it was time to do the right thing and get things in order. My relationship with God grew stronger and I knew He will make a way when there is no way. Our purpose was to go through to get to know each other because we forgot that part from some time. We had to start compromising and started considering each need and wants. Putting ourselves in each

As the Lies Turn

other shoes made us realize how selfish and stubborn we have been. We gave each other our all and released the hurt and letting go of the past. Some people may feel that what we endured was too much handle, but every situation is different. Women and men have different tolerance level and can tolerate whatever they can. Once we agreed to let God handle our battles and let God work it out, we knew we will be in our marriage for the long haul. We made another vow to be devoted, faithful, honest, encouraging, putting one another first, trustworthy and have open communication. I surrendered my mind from evil thoughts and what if's.

FORGIVENESS

"Forgiveness is God's grace extended to the undeserving"

As the Lies Turn

What if our marriage doesn't work out after going through? What if we just doing this marriage for everyone else? What if the playing of games not over? All these questions, I had to lay to rest before it damaged anything, I was pushing forward to be a happy couple. The time came for me to take everything in that I prayed for. Often, I will pray for things to change and then question God when God move on His time. It was not about me anymore, rather it was more about the fight that I had in me to help my marriage. Fighting for what's right and giving our hearts, soul and mind to one another and God. It was a blessing in

As the Lies Turn

disguise to overcome the obstacles that were thrown at our union. We have been talked about, misled and lied on. No weapon form against us shall prosper. Keeping God first is our goal to continue to strive for unity in our marriage. The two will become one flesh. We must be as one, act as one and deliver as one. We began to start dating each other again. Marriage is not a contract or a piece of paper, it's a covenant. Ephesians 4-2:3 "With all humility and gentleness with patience, bearing with one another in love, eager to maintain the unity of the Spirit in the bond of peace".

Prayers Turns Table

When I say we serve a great God that's just
what I meant. Who would have thought that
two stubborn people can come to agreement
to work it out? Prayers change everything,
no matter the situation. Being in the dark
space and not knowing if we will ever see
the light God saw fit that we didn't see. It
did not happen overnight. It took some time
and understanding to make sure that the
steps that God led my husband was the best.
God didn't come when I needed him to but

showed up on His time. God timing is the best time because you will never know when, but He will surely fix what you have prayed for.

PRAYER

Psalm 5:3

"In the morning, O LORD, you hear my voice; in the morning I lay my requests before and wait in expectation"

As the Lies Turn

I always put Him first and everything I ever

prayed for, He made sure it came to life. I

just talked to God and let him know

everything I wanted for my marriage and if

it was meant to be. God saw fit to bless our

union because of the love we had for each

other and God knew we needed each other.

During difficult times I praise Him. I praised

Him when I was up and even when I was

down. I lift Him up no matter the storm I

was going through and been through. I

talked to God and asked him for guidance

and to lead our marriage in the right

direction. I prayed to protect us against lust, temptation, and wrong doings. Pray against the enemy because when you are happy, he comes to kill, steal and destroy. I serve a great God and I know through trials that I must keep faith and stay prayed up. When I was in deep prayer, I would start crying because I know God had release a lot of burdens off of me. He told me to trust Him in everything He does and not to lose sight. The time I spent with God was to endure the overflow of great things that was about to happen. My relationship with God is wonderful because He knew what I needed before I prayed for it. I ask God to let me

As the Lies Turn

stay focus and keep my eyes on Him and my marriage. When God moved, it was unexpectedly even when I didn't deserve it. Although, during the test, I never gave up because I knew there was hope at the end of my battle. His love and grace God made me realize that He never leaves me nor forsake me. The battle was not ours but of the Lord. Prayer: I come to you as humble as I know how to not ask for anything but to thank you for what you have already done, going to do and will continue to do. You know what is needed and you know my heart. I have been lost and my mistakes shouldn't weigh heavy on my heart. I'm sorry for all the wrongs

As the Lies Turn

I've done and put you through. Lord I am

sorry for taking everything I encounter for

granted. Lord, forgive me for I am your

child. You showed us how to forgive

because you have forgiven us for our sins.

We are not perfect, but you are perfect to us.

I thank you for setting me free from the

bondage of my bitterness towards my

husband. Jesus name, Amen.

As the Lies Turn

Life of a New Beginning

God had to crush us to mend our

brokenness. Love will break you down, but

when God closes one door, He opens

another one. Challenge equals change and

you must be prepared for a challenge in

order to effect a change. It's a new

beginning for me in many ways. Through

our journey, we've come to realize how to

have a successful marriage. We know

through years we will still have

disagreements and we are up for what God

has in store for us. We learned to talk

As the Lies Turn

everything out and not hold anything in. The love we desire from each other now is a great blessing. We lost hope before, but now expressing our feelings and being open to each other is a huge step for both of us. Communication is the number one key to a successful marriage. We didn't realize that in the beginning of our marriage until we came across unreasonable expectations. Now God works in our favor. Psalms 1 26:3 "Lord has done great things for us and we are filled with joy." That verse speaks for itself because God has deliverance in our destiny. God didn't have to change our marriage around, but He did, and we will

92

As the Lies Turn

praise him in our house. Thinking about the hurt, I never tried to change him, I just loved him. The beginning of our 7-year chapter was to walk in His word, to honor and obey God. Being opened to change and making sacrifices is a must. Look to God for confirmation in the decisions you make as one. The power of God's pleasure gives us joy of the Lord and that's our strength. Love is not about I give, and you get back, rather it's about loving and being genuine without the expectation to want anything in return.

Issues are self-induced and the devil is always at play. Dust off your weapons

As the Lies Turn

because the fight is on. You have the authority to defeat the devil in your marriage. Stop being afraid of the devil because your marriage will be what God says it is. Release your grudges, guard your attitude, fight with your heart, and take a risk in life. Love through God and be happy in your marriage. Everyone heard the saying Happy Wife = Happy Life, but I believe that if both parties are happy that's the key to many years of happiness. It should never be one sided all the time because we miss the picture of the man's needs as well. It states that wives need

As the Lies Turn

in a marriage are affection, conversation, honesty,

financial support and family commitment.

NEW BEGINNINGS

As the Lies Turn

2 Corinthians 5:17

"Therefore, if anyone is in Christ, the new creation has come, the old has gone, the new is here"

As the Lies Turn

It states that husbands' needs in a marriage
are sexual pleasure, appreciation, domestic
support, praise and admiration, and
attractive spouse. Love is an action word,
nothing is taken into consideration when you
don't put action to loving on your spouse. I
remember before that my husband and I did
not ever kiss each other before leaving the
house, but after a talk, we started showing
more affection towards each other. Marriage
is what you make it to be. If you believe it
will be hard then it will be. It you believe it
will be easy and fun, then it will be. We

As the Lies Turn

made it work for us and what fit us as

husband and wife. We kept God first and

communicated effectively and this is our life

of a new beginning and 7 years of marital

bliss. God did it!

As the Lies Turn

My Unexpected Gift from God

Shyly Hearing Every Masculine Amazing and
Intelligent Attractive but Hot voice.

My mind reached for this Athletic, Nice and Tall
Handsome Overly Naughty yet

Charming and Obedient Loving while being an
Excellent Man giving me Awesome but Nurturing

Conversations over the phone.

Thinking of my unexpected Gift from God

I allowed my heart to be happily opened and put
back together.

God has sent me love and he was amazing, and not
perfect and has flaws that allowed me

to help better him

Feeling my unexpected Gift from God

As the Lies Turn

Learning Anthony has been raw and fun, peaceful and young, sadness and joy.

I needed help with allowing my heart to open and release my past.

My heart was so broken it was so hard to trust

But today moving forward I am open to

My Unexpected Gift from God!

56556722R00062

Made in the USA
Columbia, SC
27 April 2019